There should bring back man
all my love
John. (Chu
x x x   x x x

WESTON-
SUPER-MARE
IN OLD PHOTOGRAPHS

WESTON-SUPER-MARE
IN OLD PHOTOGRAPHS

COLLECTED BY
SHARON POOLE

ALAN SUTTON

Alan Sutton Publishing Limited
Phoenix Mill · Far Thrupp · Stroud · Gloucestershire

First published 1987

Reprinted 1993

British Library Cataloguing in Publication Data

Weston-Super-Mare in old photographs.
1. Weston-Super-Mare (Somerset) — History
I. Poole, Sharon
942.3'96   DA690.W53

ISBN 0–86299–417–9

Typesetting and origination by
Alan Sutton Publishing Limited.
Printed in Great Britain by
WBC Limited, Bridgend.

CONTENTS

This peaceful scene was photographed in 1932 and originally entitled 'Sunshine in Winter'.
The mother and her son are seated in the Art Deco style entrance to the Winter Gardens.

INTRODUCTION

Weston-super-Mare developed from a tiny fishing village into a large Victorian town and seaside resort in just over one hundred and fifty years. For at least the last hundred years its growth has been recorded by the camera.

The first photographer arrived in the area in 1847. However, at this date the trade was in portraiture or 'photographic likenesses' as they were then known. In 1849 Mr Sharpe advertised a 'Photographic Portrait Room' which was situated opposite the Independent Chapel in the High Street. The site is now occupied by Samuel's shop. Ten years later photography was still being compared with painting as J. Purnell advertised as a 'Photographic Artist' again working from the High Street. Often these early photographers were seasonal visitors, operating for two or three months in the town and then travelling on. By 1887 the camera had ceased being regarded as a novelty and Weston had five resident photographers, the number growing to thirteen by 1911. Two of the better known photographers in the town in the closing years of the last century were the Davies brothers. An album of their pictures of the family and town still survives. Apart from such interesting scenes as the laying of the tram tracks in 1902 and the building of the Grand Pier the following year, it includes some enchanting family shots of picnics on the beach and the children with their toys.

As a holiday resort, Weston-super-Mare has naturally been captured on plate or film many times, and although the majority of views are centred on the seafront or beach, there survive a great variety of inland scenes. These range from family snapshots through photographic postcards to professional views taken by such masters as Francis Frith and F.R. Bedford.

The selection of photographs I have chosen ranges over a period of nearly one hundred years beginning from the late 1860s and finishing about 1959. In the earliest views one can still detect a hint of the wild untamed aspect the shore presented to the first visitors early in the nineteenth century. These visitors would mostly have been artists, or convalescents, tired of the social round at Bath or Clifton and attracted by the sea air and spectacular sunsets. Indeed there was little else to attract anyone at that date. As Thomas Turner put it in a letter written in 1815, 'Weston is a very small village, consisting, I suppose, of not more than thirty houses; the majority of these are new, indeed, I may say built within the past ten years'.

The local Lords of the Manor, the Pigott family of Brockley, near Bristol, had a summer residence at Grove House (in what is now Grove Park) and it was this family, as the largest landowners, that was one of the driving forces behind Weston's later development. Building started on the first hotel in 1808 and growth and change have taken place at a rapid rate ever since. Milestones in Weston's history such as the arrival of Brunel's Bristol & Exeter Railway have unfortunately gone unrecorded by the camera but we are luckier in later events. The new pier at Birnbeck was photographed shortly after its opening in 1867. Pictures also survive of such occasions as the opening of Knightstone Baths in 1902 and the opening of the Winter Gardens and Pavilion in 1927 as well as many other events in the annals of the town. All these are featured within this book.

From the 1850s large areas of land were released for development. Select housing estates were built on the hillsides – Montpelier and the Shrubbery are two of these. Here, large detached villas housed the growing middle-classes, anxious to display their often newly-acquired wealth for all to see. Access to these estates was usually via a toll gate with attached lodge, in order to keep out uninvited visitors! The Shrubbery gate was still in use in 1930.

To the south of the town builders concentrated on lower middle-class semi-detached housing. Solidly built, these houses have a unique character, often displaying individual architectural details of great charm. They were almost a mirror of the family within – a unified front masking their individuality.

As tourism grew in importance to Weston-super-Mare, so the large villas lining the seafront were gradually converted into hotels and boarding houses and by the 1890s Weston was totally holiday orientated. With the town's expansion shops and businesses opened to cater for the new residents and visitors. Photographs of these premises, sometimes with the staff proudly lined up outside the door, are fascinating studies in social history on their own account. Usually specialising in one particular type of ware, photographs of these shops also record disappearing trades. Grocers, gentlemen's outfitters, off-licences and toy shops might all be familiar today, but hosiers, dyers, tea dealers and saddlers? These have all but disappeared. Competitions for window displays, often sponsored by manufac-turers, have sometimes resulted in some unusual pictures as winning entrants had their work photographed for posterity.

Like many towns in the 1980s, Weston-super-Mare is still growing. Large super stores are being built around Winterstoke Road (once the old railway branch line into the town) and vast new housing estates are covering the fields around the outskirts of Weston at Worle and Locking Castle. All this building probably seems as controversial today as the developments of the nineteenth century must have appeared to the original villagers of Weston. The new Royal Life development, due to start in 1987, will bring further alterations to the face that Weston presents to its 60,000 residents and seasonal influx of 350,000 holiday makers.

It is, of course, easy to wallow in the nostalgia of old photographs. To see only the pretty costume, picturesque fishing boats and quaint shops. Life naturally had its harder side. Unemployment could be just as much a spectre in Victorian times (and was in the 1930s) as today and closer inspection of views of some of the poorer parts of the town may show ragged-looking children or weary street vendors.

When I was asked to compile this book I gave a lot of thought as to which photographs I wanted to use. Some favourites are featured. Although these may have been published before, I make no excuse for including them here as I feel no book of photographs of old Weston would be complete without them. The child building a sand castle (or is it a mud pie?) in the High Street is one of these, as is the evocative scene of two boatmen leaning on a flatner in Knightstone Harbour. However I have also tried to find some more unusual or early views. The fine photograph of a family in the garden of their Montpelier villa is more reminiscent of perhaps Cheltenham or Clifton than Weston, and the photographs of the lanes and courts around Carlton Street are the only surviving record of this complex of artisans' cottages built in the 1840s. They are pictured shortly before their demolition in 1961 as part of the post-war 'slum clearance' schemes then in vogue.

The street scenes often repay more than a superficial glance with interesting detail. The most immediately noticeable differences from today are the gas lighting, the often unsurfaced road and the lavish amount of greenery. The latter has been eroded as front gardens and hedges have given way to car parking, and grass verges and trees have sometimes been lost in street widening schemes as the age of the motor car made itself felt. Some of Weston's larger landmarks have been demolished to make way for even larger landmarks! Glentworth Hall, Villa Rosa, Etonhurst and Worthy Lodge are just a few of the substantial early Victorian properties that have been replaced with apartment blocks.

Transport of the past is always an interesting subject and Weston-super-Mare's role as a tourist resort gave public transport an especially important part to play. Holiday makers would normally arrive by train before the days of universal car ownership. Once established in their lodgings they could choose from an extraordinary variety of vehicles in which to travel. Donkey chairs provided a taxi service for lone travellers, whilst wagonettes and trams catered for town trips. Donkeys, pony carts and goat carts were available for beach rides. Excursions further afield could be by horse brake and, later on, by charabanc and for journeys along the coast or across the Bristol Channel, paddle steamers operated regularly from Birnbeck Pier.

People's memories will fade and paintings depend so much upon the artist's interpretation and skill that photographs are unique in the record that they preserve. The camera never lies as the saying goes. I hope you will now go on to receive as much enjoyment from this book as I have had in its compilation.

Sharon Poole 1987

BARBARA SYDENHAM AND HER SISTER, pictured in a goat cart around 1870. For this studio photograph, J.G. Williams, the photographer, probably borrowed the cart with its attendant boy, from the beach, where they were a common sight at this date.

SECTION ONE

The Town

JUBILEE ROAD looking towards Baker Street c. 1919. Jubilee Garage is on the left.

A VIEW OF THE TOWN FROM WORLEBURY IRON AGE HILLFORT, the collapsed stone ramparts of which can be glimpsed bottom left. The wide sweep of the bay is uninterrupted by the Grand Pier which was built some twenty years after this 1880s photograph was taken.

ROYAL CRESCENT pictured in the late 1870s. This fine Crescent was built in 1847.

This picture, taken from the seafront in the 1870s, shows the rear of the Royal Hotel with Royal Terrace on the left.

HOUSES UNDER CONSTRUCTION IN THE BOULEVARD, 1887. The buildings seen across the field are those in Alfred Street.

SOUTH PARADE UNDER SNOW on 16 March 1887, as photographed by Robert Cox of Victoria Lodge.

THIS VIEW OVER WESTON WAS TAKEN FROM SOUTH ROAD. The turreted building is the Shrubbery water tower, originally built to provide a water supply to Villa Rosa. The curving road in the foreground was the old access to the Shrubbery estate before Shrubbery Avenue was linked to Atlantic Road in 1871 via a toll gate.

VILLA ROSA c. 1912. The Crouch family relax as the gardener mows the lawn.

THE CARRIAGE DRAWS UP to the front door of Villa Rosa, c. 1912. Mr Stephens was the coachman. The coachhouse survives today as Villa Rosetta.

THE INNER HALL AT VILLA ROSA photographed c. 1912.

THE GARDENER'S COTTAGE, VILLA ROSA. Later known as East Lodge, this pretty pebbledash cottage was built between 1841 and 1846, to house the gardener for the Villa Rosa estate. In this 1911 photograph, Mr Daffern is standing on the left with his wife Emily, daughter Catherine, aged 2, and son Thomas. The cottage was situated at the end of Shrubbery Avenue.

SHRUBBERY MEWS, UPPER CHURCH ROAD. In recent years the building, somewhat altered, was used as Shrubbery Garage. It was demolished in 1986.

THE SHRUBBERY TOLL GATE IN SHRUBBERY AVENUE, pictured in 1930. This was built in 1871. Residents of the estate paid 15s (75p) a year to cover tolls. Others paid 4d (2p) for a motorcar or taxi, 3d (1½p) for a horse-drawn vehicle and 1d (½p) for a person on foot or horseback.

OVERVALE, MONTPELIER. One of Weston's fine Victorian villas built in the 1860s. Around 1930, Henry Butt, Weston's well-known property developer and the town's first mayor, bought the house and converted it into flats. In this view Theodor James and his family are photographed in their garden c. 1871.

THE GATE LODGE at Montpelier, 1870.

This picture was taken c. 1894, from the top of the Town Quarry, looking down Queens Road. The old track known as Quarry Road can still be seen running parallel on the left of the new road.

DEMOLITION OF SPRING COTTAGE, High Street, 1871. The house had been built for Cornelius Hancock. It was described as having sliding green Venetian shutters, with tea-plant and roses over the door. It was fronted by a very long garden. On the left of this picture is Jesse Shorney, builder, who had the demolition contract. The buildings in the background are those of South Parade.

THIS BUNGALOW-STYLE HOUSE was situated in Regent Street facing south, between the Beach Hotel and Wellington Place. It was occupied for many years by a barrister, Guy Phillips, seen here with his wife, c. 1867. The building was demolished after his death in the mid 1870s.

LITCHFIELD HOUSE IN REGENT STREET, was the residence of Captain H.T. Gammel R N. Captain Gammel was well-known for his habit of presenting a pair of gloves to each of the local cabmen every Christmas. On his death the house was sold to Mr Macfarlane who demolished it and built the Bungalow Hotel in 1905. The site is now occupied by the Grand Central Hotel, built in 1925.

AN 1860S PHOTOGRAPH OF WHEREAT'S PUBLIC LIBRARY AND READING ROOM. This was on the corner of Regent Street and Beach Road.

WESTON-SUPER-MARE LIBRARY AND MUSEUM, the Boulevard, c. 1911. This was one of the last public buildings to be designed by local architect Hans Price. It opened in 1900.

WESTON-SUPER-MARE MUSEUM, 1906, with curator W.H. Palmer. The Museum was situated on the upper floor of the Library building until 1975 when it was moved to its present home in Burlington Street.

THE PUBLIC LIBRARY ON EASTER TUESDAY 1906. Librarian and Curator W.H. Palmer is in the centre with Stanley Pollard on the right. The latter died in the following year, aged 22.

LOWER CHURCH ROAD about 1900.

A VIEW LOOKING EAST ALONG SOUTHSIDE c. 1905. A milkman is standing beside his cart in the distance whilst, on the left, a boy is using a wooden yoke to carry milkcans.

TRAFALGAR COTTAGE, BRISTOL ROAD, was the home of the YMCA in Weston. In this 1890s view, Ross & Co's mineral water manufactory can be seen on the left.

THIS LATER VIEW OF THE YMCA shows some substantial changes to the building. An extra storey has been added and bay windows built.

WEST LODGE, BRISTOL ROAD, 1897. This was one of two gatehouses to the Lodge, a large mansion built in 1863 for the eighth Earl of Cavan. The Lodge was demolished in 1977 but the gatehouses survive.

BRISTOL ROAD IN THE 1890s. The Cemetery Lodge can be glimpsed through the trees on the left. The houses on the right are in Eastfield Park.

'PEAK WINA'. This cairn is situated in Weston Woods. It is said that, years ago, fishermen on their way over the hill to tend their nets at Birnbeck used to throw stones on the cairn for good luck.

ASHCOMBE LODGE, 1885. This tiny gamekeeper's cottage was situated in Bristol Road, on the corner of Wood Lane. It was demolished in 1890.

THE TOWN HALL AND EMMANUEL CHURCH pictured c. 1870. The Town Hall was built in 1856 on land donated to the town by Henry Davies.

THE TOWN HALL was considerably altered and enlarged in 1897 as this picture shows. The gas lamp in the road has a fine circular horse trough around its base.

THE ENTRANCE TO THE SUMMER AND WINTER GARDENS in the Boulevard c. 1909. This building later became the Tivoli Theatre. It suffered severe bomb damage in 1942 and the site is now occupied by Tivoli Court flats.

LOOKING EAST ALONG WATERLOO STREET, c. 1910. The spire of Christ Church can just be seen in the distance.

GLEBE ROAD pictured c. 1911. The man on the left appears to be selling rabbits from his cart.

THREE CHILDREN LINE UP FOR THIS PHOTOGRAPH OF PALMER STREET, c. 1910.

STANLEY GROVE ROAD. A cul-de-sac of neat, respectable Victorian villas.

A RATHER DIFFERENT HOME HERE in the shape of Langport House, Eastfield Park. This ornate building was the residence of Henry Butt, the town's first mayor. Mr Butt can be seen standing on the verandah.

65 *WESTON-SUPER-MARE. — Regent Street. — LL*

A VIEW OF REGENT STREET looking towards the seafront, c. 1910. The Shaftesbury Commercial Temperance Hotel is on the left, whilst the Railway Hotel (now the Quantocks) can be seen behind the wagonette.

ANOTHER VIEW OF REGENT STREET, this time looking east in the 1890s. The building with the tower was the Wesleyan Chapel on the corner of St James Street.

OXFORD STREET looking towards the seafront, C. 1911. A tram is approaching although a cart appears to be obstructing the rails.

ST JAMES STREET, C. 1913.

ST MARGARET'S IN QUEENS ROAD, was a Holy Family Home for orphans and children in care. The house was built in 1879.

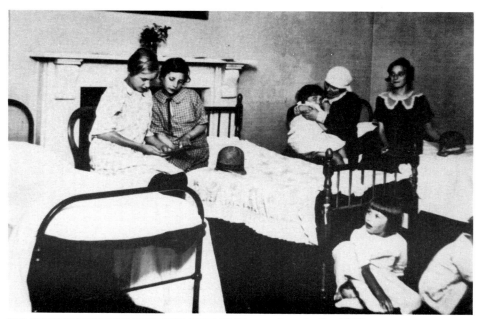

ONE OF THE DORMITORIES AT ST MARGARET'S HOME seen here in the 1920s.

MEADOW STREET, C. 1957. The turning on the right is the High Street, with Regent Street ahead.

JOYCE MULLINS (right) and her cousin Kathleen Payne, cycling in Burlington Street in 1938.

CARLTON STREET in 1958. The Prince Of Wales public house still stands as does the Salvation Army Citadel which is the large building in the centre. All the other buildings have been demolished.

SIDMOUTH COTTAGES WEST, 1958. This area was demolished in 1961 for the Dolphin Square development.

Seafront and Beach

THE WILMOT FAMILY on the beach at Anchor Head c. 1880.

THIS VIEW OF GLENTWORTH BAY was taken in the late 1870s. The large house on the left is Glentworth Hall, demolished in the 1970s to make way for a block of flats. You can see here the natural pebble beach that existed before Marine Lake was built.

A VIEW OF WESTON FROM BEACH ROAD taken c. 1890, before the Grand Pier was built.

KNIGHTSTONE ROAD C. 1903. This little girl must surely have been wearing her best hat for this photograph beside the flatner 'Diamond Jubilee'.

TWO LADIES STROLL ACROSS KNIGHTSTONE ROAD. The photograph was taken from the downstairs window of No.8 Manilla Crescent, in the 1890s.

PADDLING near the Grand Pier in 1904. The pier had only just been built.

MORE PADDLERS, this time beside Birnbeck Pier. The switchback and waterchute can clearly be seen on the pier.

AN EARLY PHOTOGRAPH OF BIRNBECK PIER taken a few years after it was built in 1867.

LOOKING LANDWARDS from under Birnbeck Pier about 1870.

THE PADDLESTEAMER *SCOTIA* draws away from Birnbeck Pier on a Channel cruise in 1901. The lifeboat house was not built in its present position until 1902. A line of fishing stakes stretch out into the water to the north.

TWO BOATMEN pause for a chat and a smoke over R. Hedge's boat *Henrietta* at Knightstone Harbour in 1904. The boat is a flatner, a local type of flat-bottomed fishing craft.

ANCHOR HEAD was always a favourite place to sit as this crowded scene, taken on the 30 August 1911, shows.

THE SANDS DAY NURSERY was set up in 1913, by two local ladies, Mrs Beatrice Jones and Mrs Edith Birch. Day trippers could leave their children there on payment of a small fee as long as the children were under five years old.

A CROWD OF CHILDREN enjoying 'Professor' Staddon's Punch and Judy show on the beach in 1932.

THERE WAS NO TRADES DESCRIPTION ACT IN THE 1890s to deter this ice cream vendor from advertising 'the best ice cream in town'!

ONE OF THE MANY BEACH STALLS that set up on the sands at the turn of the century. This one is selling mineral waters and teas.

ANCHOR HEAD, 1896. A local fishing boat or 'flatner' prepares to board passengers for a trip around the bay. The building above is the Royal Pier Hotel. Fishing nets are drying over the wall.

THE BURNELL FAMILY pose in this delightful donkey cart on the beach in 1896.

on the sands, Weston

THE SAME CART APPEARS AGAIN IN THIS PHOTOGRAPH of c. 1904. The children have come prepared for their day on the sands, with buckets and wooden spades.

SAND SCULPTURE ON THE BEACH. This work was entitled *The Last Message* and depicted a scene from the Boer War.

BATHERS photographed on the 4 August 1918. William Youle is marked with an X.

Hotels and Restaurants

THIS MAN IS PROBABLY MR EVANS with his dog, outside the Grove Park Restaurant at 88 High Street c. 1912.

THE ROYAL PIER HOTEL under proprietor, Frederick Harris, in the 1870s. In 1872 Mr Harris was advertising the hotel with 'private sea baths, coffee rooms, good stabling and coach houses and spacious dining room'. Board and lodging cost from £1 10s (£1.50p) per week.

THE GRAND ATLANTIC HOTEL photographed in the 1890s. Originally built as a school, the building was enlarged and converted into an hotel in 1889. Compare this picture with one of The College on page 78.

THE PLOUGH HOTEL was one of the earliest inns in the town. Situated in the High Street, it was mentioned in the 1822 guide to Weston as being a 'comfortable house'. It is pictured here in the 1930s just after being sold. It was demolished in order to enlarge Marks and Spencer's new store.

AN ADVERTISEMENT FOR THE CORFIELD BOARDING HOUSE at 38 Birnbeck Road, from a 1920s town guide.

VIEWS OF THE INTERIOR OF BROWN BROTHERS CAFE c. 1910.

THE CASTLE CAFE was in Castle Street, one of the many lanes off Carlton Street. This whole area was demolished in the post-war clearance scheme in 1961. Dolphin Square and the Carlton Street car park now occupy the site.

THE BELLE VUE RESTAURANT in the High Street, pictured about 1904. The site is now occupied by Dixons Photographic Shop.

THE LOUNGE, HOTEL MEDINA, Royal Crescent.

THE RIDEN FAMILY pose for a picture outside their home at 62 Orchard Street. Mr Riden (not seen here) was a coach painter and sign writer, whilst his wife ran this apartment house.

WESTON=SUPER=MARE.

Furnished
Apartments.

LOFTY AND HEALTHY
5 ROOMS.
PERFECT SANITATION.

ON THE SEA FRONT,
Facing the Atlantic, but Sheltered from the North and East Winds.

Near Madeira Cove,
Overlooking Anchor Head
and Glentworth Bay.

Within a Few Minutes' Walk of the Pier
and the unrivalled Woods of Weston
(400 acres).

**N.B. The Temperature of this particular part of Weston-Super-Mare is
Several Degrees Warmer than many Inland Winter Resorts.**

FOR INCLUSIVE TERMS apply:

Mrs. F. G. READ, 7, Claremont Crescent.

AN ADVERTISEMENT FOR FURNISHED APARTMENTS to let in Claremont Crescent, from a town guide of the 1920s.

SECTION FOUR

Transport

THE BRISTOL TRAMWAYS & CARRIAGE COMPANY, Limited.
WESTON-SUPER-MARE BRANCH.

The Company's

BLUE MOTOR TAXI-CABS

may be obtained at each of the Public Stands for Long or Short Journeys.

—ON HIRE,—
PRIVATE

Touring Cars,

by the Day, Week, Month or Year.

During the Summer months the Company run

HIGH-CLASS————

Torpedo Motor Charabancs

TO

Cheddar, Wells, Glastonbury, Minehead, Holford Combe,

and many other Interesting and Historic Places around WESTON-SUPER-MARE.

For Accessories, Repairs, Petrol, Tyres, &c., go to the Company's Garage, Neva Road, near G.W. Railway.

OPEN DAY AND NIGHT.

CENTRAL BOOKING OFFICE: ENTRANCE GRAND PIER.

Tel. 110 (2 Lines).

Telegrams :
" Cab," Weston-super-Mare.

Address all Enquiries :

W. J. GREEN, Local Manager,
Office and Garage, **22, Beach Road.**

THIS ADVERTISEMENT FOR BRISTOL TRAMWAYS' CHARABANCS AND TAXIS appeared in the 1925 Town Guide. The Company was formed in Bristol in 1874 but it was not until 1910 that they began to operate services in Weston, starting with their Blue Motor Taxi Cabs. Their first regular bus service in the town began in 1912.

THE WORKING MENS UNIONIST CLUB prepare to leave from Alexandra Parade for their annual outing. The vehicle was hired from the Bristol Tramways & Carriage Company.

MOGG'S BAND in a Bristol Tramways & Carriage Company charabanc between 1914 and 1916. They are parked outside St Pauls Church.

BURNELL'S GARAGE AND DEPOT in Knightstone Road, pictured in the late 1920s. The large building is the Glentworth Hall Hotel, now demolished. Among the outings advertised are trips to Cheddar, Clevedon and Burrington for which prices range from 3s (15p) to 4s6d [22½p].

MILTON ROAD GARAGE, c. 1922. Three charabancs are parked here whilst their passengers enjoy the beach.

LAYING THE TRAM TRACKS at the junction of Oxford Street and Beach Road, 1902.

TRAM NO.1 waits at the Sanatorium terminus. As you can see, not an inch of advertising space was wasted. Even the backs of the swing-over seats bore enamel signs. The picture was taken c. 1920.

INTERIOR OF THE TRAMWAYS CAR SHED, probably about 1910. The hand-pushed tower wagon can be seen on the extreme right. This was used for repairing the overhead wires.

WESTON-SUPER-MARE TRAMWAYS STAFF lined up in front of a 'toast-rack' tram in the car shed c. 1909.

A DERAILED TRAM in Locking Road, awaits the repair crew, 22 June 1934.

THE TRAM MEETS COMPETITION in the form of a motor bus in this 1930 view of Knightstone Road.

WESTON'S SECOND RAILWAY STATION, about 1870. The first station was a small terminus at the end of a branch line from the main Bristol & Exeter Railway. The station soon became too small and this new station was built in 1866, on the site now occupied by Tesco's store.

WESTON'S THIRD AND PRESENT RAILWAY STATION, pictured soon after its opening on 1 March 1884. This was the first station in the town to be linked directly with the main line via a loop into the town.

THE STATION GOODS YARD from the top of Lalonde's building in Station Road, photographed about 1930. The building in the background is the 1866 passenger station which was turned over to goods use when the new station opened in 1884.

'TERRIER' TANK ENGINE NO.4 hauls a Clevedon-bound train out from the Light Railway station in Ashcombe Road, about 1938.

ONE OF WESTON'S DONKEY CHAIRS. These were hired like taxis, but were only suitable for one person.

WILLIAM PARSONS with his donkey chair on the beach. The names of the family are not known. They were photographed c. 1890.

THIS SMART TURNOUT WAS KNOWN AS 'THE WESTON WONDER'. A common sight in the town for many years during the 1870s, it is reputed that they could reach a speed of 13 mph, once running from Bristol to Weston in one hour. The driver is William White, veterinary surgeon and farrier (a useful combination at those speeds!). In the background is John Bath who was proprietor of the Railway Hotel (now the Quantocks) from 1861 to 1873.

DONKEY WHEELCHAIR MEN, probably pictured in South Parade. The men are believed to include Messrs Atherton, Cribb, Legg, Marshman, Attwell, Brewer, Hall and Sam Hawkins.

THE HORSE BUS belonging to the Weston & Clevedon Light Railway passes the Big Lamp on its way to the Light Railway Station in Ashcombe Road c. 1905.

S. COLES WITH HIS FOUR-IN-HAND. Pictured outside his fishmonger's premises in Meadow Street.

A GREAT WESTERN RAILWAY CART in Moorland Road in 1902. The carter is S. Williams.

THE FIRST STEAM LORRY IN WESTON. This vehicle was instrumental in persuading the GWR to replace the Clevedon Road level crossing with a bridge.

Steamer at Grand Pier Weston-Super-Mare.

PADDLESTEAMER *DEVONIA* at the Grand Pier landing stage. She was one of the very few steamers ever to berth at the Grand Pier. Despite the landing jetty being especially long to land boats at all tides, the strong currents made mooring dangerous. The extension was removed in 1916.

PASSENGERS DISEMBARKING FROM A STEAMER after a wet and windy excursion to Ilfracombe from Weston c. 1923.

AN AVRO BIPLANE on the 'Aviation Ground' on 27 September 1919. This appears to be a field somewhere near Uphill.

WESTON AIRPORT in 1937. This photograph was used by Western Airways for their publicity brochure that year. They leased the airfield which was opened in June 1936.

SECTION FIVE

Schools

A CLASS AT CHRIST CHURCH INFANT SCHOOL c. 1910. This school was opened in 1874 to serve the rapidly growing area around Baker Street and Swiss Road.

GIRLS AT LOCKING ROAD SCHOOL C. 1906.

A VERY DIFFERENT CLASS here from the one above. An algebra lesson at Carlton House School for girls, c. 1905. This school, situated in Connaught Place, was run by the Misses Watkins and Ashby.

WESTON SECONDARY SCHOOL NETBALL TEAM with Headmistress, Miss Farthing.

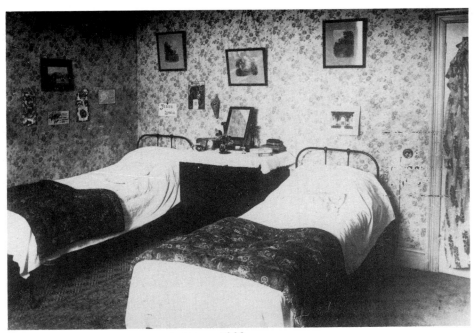

A BEDROOM AT CARLTON HOUSE SCHOOL, C. 1903.

THE COLLEGE, IN BEACH ROAD, was built in 1854 for Jonathan Elwell. Later run by Dr Nunn, the school was finally converted into an hotel, the Grand Atlantic, which opened in 1889. (see page 52).

SYDNEY HOUSE SCHOOL, Edinburgh Place, 1892. This private school for boys was run by Miss Katharine Dixon. The group of pupils here include Arthur Stanley Eddington (back left), who went on to become a world famous astronomer. A plaque on the wall of 'Varzin' in Walliscote Road commemorates his boyhood home.

The College,
Weston=super=Mare.

THE

ANIDJAH FIRE ESCAPE DRILL.

FIRE DRILL at the College, c. 1903.

JOHN HODGE receives his prize at St Peter's School sports day, 1936.

MILTON SCHOOL OF GARDENING was run by Miss Gandy and Fraülein Klausman, to teach young ladies the art of fruit and vegatable growing. It was situated at The Grove, Milton.

SECTION SIX

Churches

THE SALVATION ARMY BAND at The Citadel in Carlton Street. This picture was taken some time before 1900.

CHRIST CHURCH IN MONTPELIER, was built in 1855. This photograph was taken in 1877 during building operations to enlarge the church.

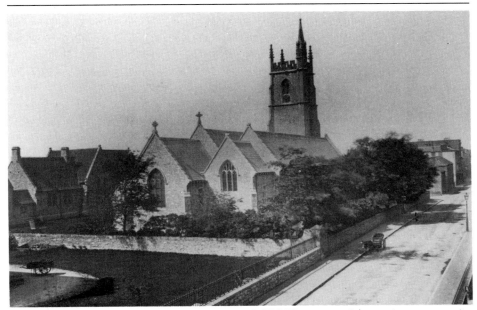

EMMANUEL CHURCH was built in 1847, at a cost of £3,200, to serve the growing community south of Regent Street. It was built by Robert Gregory, a local builder. This view was taken some time before 1902 when tram tracks were laid in Oxford Street.

ALL SAINTS CHURCH. Who would recognise this rural scene as being in the heart of Weston? This building was replaced between 1898 and 1902 by a fine stone church designed by the Royal Academician, C.F. Bodley FSA.

'CUTTING THE SOD CEREMONY' at St Pauls Church on 11 May 1911

THE INTERIOR OF ST PAULS CHURCH, shortly after its opening.

WADHAM STREET BAPTIST CHURCH pictured in the 1870s. This church was built in 1864 to a design by Hans Price, a well-known local architect. It was gutted in 1942 by enemy action but the façade remained and it was rebuilt soon after the war.

BRISTOL ROAD BAPTIST CHURCH. Another church designed by Hans Price, it was completed in 1866 at a cost of £3,000. This view was taken c. 1903.

THE VICTORIA METHODIST CHURCH was opened in 1900. This building was devastated by fire in February 1934 and the present building was erected two years later.

SECTION SEVEN

Shops

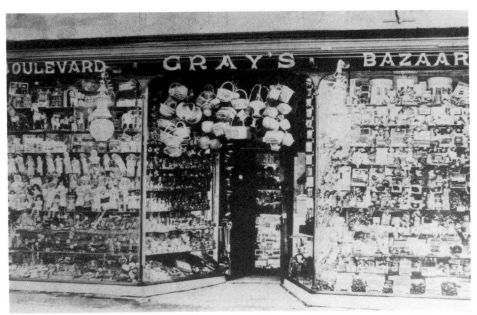

GRAY'S BAZAAR in the High Street appears to have been an Aladdin's cave for children and adults alike. The goods on display in the window include a Noah's ark, dolls, toy yachts, trumpets, train sets, baskets, pipes and walking sticks.

F.T. FORTT'S BOOT AND SHOE SHOP, 84 High Street *c*. 1912. Prices of the goods range from
1*s*11*d* to 4*s*11*d* (24p).

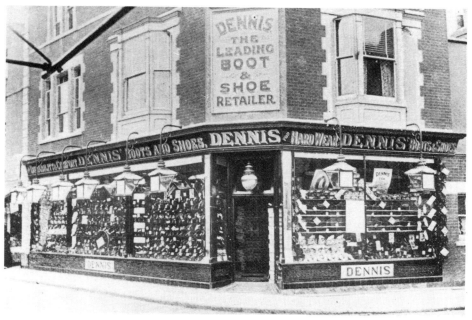

DENNIS'S BOOT STORES at 55 Meadow Street, *c*. 1910.

A PROMOTIONAL WINDOW DISPLAY for Swan inks and pens, in Davies Brothers' stationer's shop, High Street, 1904.

THE INTERIOR OF PHILLPUTS STATIONER'S SHOP at 28 High Street. Among the large selection of goods on sale is Moorcroft Pottery (in the glass display case), Meccano sets, albums, calendars, paintings, frames and desk furniture. The photograph was taken at some time before 1925.

MR PROSSER'S SADDLERY SHOP at 14 Oxford Street, c. 1920. John Prosser is seen here with his son Kenneth. The shop was demolished in the Dolphin Square development in 1961.

FRANK WITT'S PAWNBROKERS AND JEWELLERS SHOP, 17 St James Street c. 1927.

MARKS & SPENCER'S BAZAAR at 56/57 High Street on 15 May 1931. This shop was rebuilt and extended shortly after this photograph was taken.

THE LADIES' FASHION DEPARTMENT at Marks & Spencer's on 31 July 1958.

MR D. ROGERS stands outside his confectioner's shop at 15 Regent Street. Ideas on healthy eating habits have certainly changed since 1958 when this photograph was taken. The sign in the lefthand window reads 'Eat more sweets, live longer'!

THIS VIEW OF THE CASTLE CYCLE MART in Walliscote Road, was taken c. 1906. Besides selling bicycles they also hired out tricycles, bicycles, prams and pushcarts, taught cycle riding and stored cycles.

THE STAFF POSE OUTSIDE LEWIS WING'S CHEMIST SHOP in the Boulevard in the 1920s.

STAFF LINE UP OUTSIDE DAVID GREIG'S BUTCHER'S SHOP in Orchard Street, on 11 April 1932. The poster over the door is advertising pork sausages at 1s (5p) per pound.

THE MILLINERY DEPARTMENT IN TREVOR'S STORE, a ladies outfitters in the High Street. This photograph was taken in the 1920s during the fashion for cloche hats.

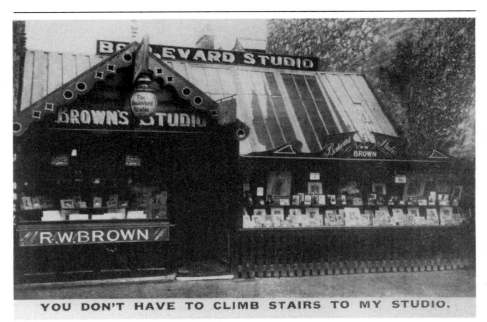

YOU DON'T HAVE TO CLIMB STAIRS TO MY STUDIO.

R.W. BROWN'S PHOTOGRAPHIC STUDIO in the Boulevard about 1920.

THE INTERIOR OF BROWN'S BOULEVARD STUDIO. The furniture is for use in portraiture. A large studio camera can be seen on the left.

SPENCER TYLER'S HIGH STREET GROCERY SHOP pictured in the 1930s shortly after being sold. On the upper floors are opticians Player-Shute, hairdresser R.V. Evans and architects Leete and Darby. On the right is the Plough Hotel.

STAFF OUTSIDE LEAVER & FOX'S HIGH STREET IRONMONGERS. The original house can still be seen above the shop. This site is now occupied by part of Woolworth's store.

BARNETT'S CYCLE AND RADIO SHOP on the corner of Alfred Street and Baker Street pictured in the 1930s.

BAKER'S FISH AND CHIP SHOP, St James Street c. 1910.

MR CATTLE'S BUTCHER'S SHOP in Meadow Street, c. 1910. This shop was on the corner of Orchard Place.

WESTON-SUPER-MARE GASLIGHT COMPANY'S SHOWROOMS at 32 Boulevard c. 1922. Messrs Priddle, Lee and Collard are standing in the doorway.

MR ADDICOTT'S SHOP on the corner of St James Street and Oxford Street, c. 1907. Note the tram tracks in Oxford Street.

MACFISHERIES SHOP in the High Street, 1958.

A WINDOW DISPLAY in George Mason's grocery shop, Meadow Street, c. 1958.

Weston at Work

MR HORRIGAN with one of his window cleaning barrows, c. 1920.

From G. COOKSLEY, House Furnisher,
20 & 22 Meadow Street, WESTON-SUPER-M
TEL. 207.

COOKSLEY'S REMOVAL VEHICLES seen here lined up for a publicity photograph in Ashcombe Road.

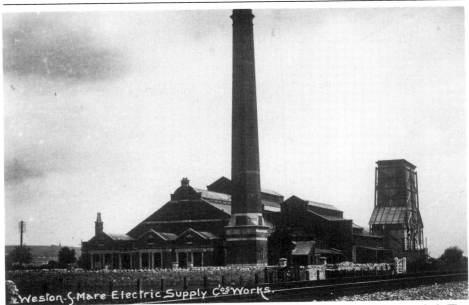

THIS PICTURE OF THE ELECTRIC SUPPLY COMPANY WORKS in Locking Road was taken c. 1912. The works opened on 24 May 1901 and were large enough to supply power to the tramways when they began operating the following year.

WORKMEN IN THE REAR COURTYARD of Weston Gaslight Company's Workshops and Stores in Burlington Street, c. 1912. This building is now the home of Woodspring Museum.

HARVESTING AT MR HUCKER'S MOORLAND FARM, Devonshire Road in the 1920s. Walter Geeve is the boy on the horse.

EDWARD J. AUSTIN, municipal worker, collecting hay from Ashcombe Park around 1930.

THE FIRST STEAM ROLLER purchased by Weston-super-Mare UDC, pictured in Severn Road in 1907. The machine was made by Aveling Porter. Sam Pike is the workman in the centre of the photograph.

RESURFACING THE HIGH STREET on 6 March 1958. The old road of wooden blocks can be seen where the surface has been stripped.

AN INTERESTING VIEW, taken in the 1890s, of the two Potteries and Brickworks in Locking Road. The row of tiny cottages on the right of the works was built about 1854, from waste bricks, to house workers.

THE OFFICES OF THE ORIGINAL POTTERY, Locking Road, in the 1890s. This was a separate firm from the Royal Pottery until 1889 when they amalgamated.

COTTAGES IN LANGFORD ROAD, purchased for the Royal Pottery to house workers, 1899. The chimneys of the works can be seen beyond the gates.

EXTRACTING CLAY at the Lower Potteries near what is now Winterstoke Road, in the 1880s.

STAFF AND EMPLOYEES OF HENRY BUTT & COMPANY, pictured in Milton Quarry on 30 March 1907.

THE LIME WORKS AT MILTON QUARRY. Weston Hill is rich in limestone building material from which most of the older houses are built.

THE COMBINED SAND-DREDGER AND OIL TANKER *PORTWAY* in Knightstone Harbour. Sand is being transferred into the lorries of George & Taylor's haulage company some time in the 1920s.

T.W. LEMON throwing a pot on the wheel at his Wesuma Art Pottery, Locking Road, in the late 1920s.

OTHER EMPLOYEES add the painted decoration to the Wesuma pots before the final firing.

MILK DELIVERY IN THE 1920s. Mr T.J. Marsh of Clarence Park Dairy is seen here in Moorland Road. Housewives would bring out jugs to be filled from the churn.

KITCHEN STAFF prepare a meal for convalescents at the Royal West of England Sanatorium. A cat is basking in the heat of the range.

THIS BREWERY DRAY BELONGED TO MR WESTCOTT who ran the Waggon & Horses Inn in Regent Street. This turnout was for a special show.

A DELIVERY OF CIDER arrives at the Bath Arms from Mr Day's farm at Wick St Lawrence. This inn was situated on the corner of Alfred Street and Baker Street.

<u>SECTION NINE</u>

Having Fun

THREE LADIES EACH TAKE A DONKEY RIDE in St Peter's School field, c. 1905. The photograph was taken by Fred Viner.

WESTON CYCLING CLUB RALLY, 1888. Weston-super-Mare Cycling Club was formed in 1878. This fascinating photograph shows riders with almost 60 cycles. Pictured in the last days of the Ordinary or 'penny farthing' bicycle, most of this type of machine are seen here with older riders. The younger members are using the new rear-drive safety cycles. There are also seven tricycles in the picture, two of which are being ridden by ladies.

CYCLING CARNIVAL IN GROVE PARK, C. 1910. These summer events were held for several years around the turn of the century. The man on the left is Charles Masters, entry No.6 is Miss Doughty with William Doughty behind her and entry No.13 is Miss E. Norvill. The canvas screens were erected to prevent anyone seeing the subsequent firework display without paying an entry fee.

THIS CARNIVAL FLOAT WON FIRST PRIZE for 'Tricycles' at the Cycling Carnival in 1892. The float is pictured in Orchard Street.

WESTON CYCLING CLUB meet on the seafront for the first run of the season, 1885.

THIS PHOTOGRAPH, ENTITLED 'SINGERS AT KNIGHTSTONE' was taken by amateur photographer W.H. James in the 1890s.

ENTITLED 'MY MONKEY', this photograph of a musician and his companion was also taken by W.H. James on the promenade at Glentworth Bay in 1896.

ROLLER SKATING ON THE GRAND PIER in 1904. Roller skating was a popular pastime in Weston from the 1870s. Besides using the Grand Pier, where certain times were reserved for this activity so as not to disturb others, there were also indoor rinks on Birnbeck Pier, at the Victoria Hall in the Boulevard and near Worthy Lodge in Bristol Road.

ICE SKATING ON THE FROZEN CLAYPITS of the Royal Pottery, Locking Road, in 1891.

AN ADVERTISEMENT FOR THE GRAND PIER PAVILION, 1906.

HERR KANDT'S GERMAN BAND was the opening attraction on the Grand Pier in 1904.

MOGGS BAND, pictured here on Knightstone in 1912, was founded in 1887 by Harry Mogg, who was also its conductor for 42 years. Starting with 16 members they began with evening concerts in Grove Park. As they became more proficient they started to enter national contests, finally winning the National Championships at Crystal Palace in 1912.

A MEET OF THE WESTON HARRIERS at Grove House, the home of the Master, Cecil Smyth Pigott, about 1885. Also in the picture is the Whip, Harry Miller (who was later killed by a fall from his horse) and his brother-in-law Harry Poole (standing).

WESTON-SUPER-MARE WATER POLO TEAM, finalists in the English Championship, 1905. In the front are Charles Stradling and A. Barnes. In the centre are F.R. Wright (treasurer), T. Thould, T. Davey, B. Dunn and H. Collins. In the back row are T. Davey sen., P. Radmilovic, H.H. Clark, Cecil Stradling and J.S. Walker.

OPENING OF THE 1927 SEASON ON THE 5 MAY, AT ASHCOMBE LADIES BOWLING CLUB. Mrs Ernest Macfarlane did the honours by bowling the jack.

A DIVING DISPLAY at the open-air pool, in the 1930s.

A VIEW OF THE INTERIOR OF THE FIRST FLOOR CAFE at the new open-air pool taken just before its opening in 1937. The photograph was taken by R.W. Brown.

As you can see from this photograph, taken c. 1925, amusement arcades are not a recent phenomenon in Regent Street!

THE INTERIOR OF A REGENT STREET AMUSEMENT ARCADE, c. 1925. Amongst the machines and games on offer are The Human Analyst, an Orchestrion, a rifle range and a Try-Your-Strength machine.

THE SKEE BALL SALOON on the Grand Pier, pictured at the end of the season on 23 September 1931.

CARLTON FREDRICKS (centre) with his pierrots at the Grove Park Pavilion in the 1920s.

GROVE PARK PAVILION. A fine day has brought crowds into Grove Park to watch the concert parties on the small open-air stage.

ASHCOMBE PARK entrance from Milton Road, in the 1920s.

ONE OF WESTON'S MANY STREET ENTERTAINERS, performing in Knightstone Road in the 1930s.

Weston at War

PLOUGHING UP THE LAWNS in front of Glebe House near Grove Park, in April 1917. This was part of the war effort to increase food production.

VOLUNTEERS TRAINING WITH BROOMSTICKS in Rogers' Field opposite the Post Office. Rifles were too precious to use for initial training purposes during World War I.

DURING BOTH WORLD WARS THE TRANS-ATLANTIC CABLE was a vital relay station for government messages. This detachment of soldiers are guarding the cable during the First World War.

A HIGH STREET QUEUE for margarine during World War I. Note the road surface of wooden blocks.

WHEN WORLD WAR I BROKE OUT, Ashcombe House was commandeered for use as a Red Cross Hospital for soldiers. Here, patients pose for a group photograph with the matron on Christmas Day 1917.

ANOTHER SCENE IN ASHCOMBE HOUSE HOSPITAL as staff and patients pause for a photograph before Christmas dinner, 1917.

CHRISTMAS DINNER is prepared at Ashcombe House Hospital, 1917.

PATIENTS AND STAFF IN THE ISOLATION WARD at Ashcombe House Hospital, 1917.

ON THE NIGHT OF 14 JANUARY 1918, Ashcombe House Hospital was badly damaged by fire. This photograph shows the scene the following morning. Damage was estimated at over £2000 but no one was hurt.

THE DEVASTATED INTERIOR AFTER THE FIRE. It was thought to have been caused by a defective chimney overheating a roof beam. Surprisingly a potted palm appears to be unscathed.

This photograph, taken in 1918, is of the field ambulance sent from London to Weston. The personnel pictured include Messrs Bailey, Cox, Tidman, Dowding, Ware, Robertson, Chapman, Wright, J. Chapman and Jones.

WOMEN MANNED THE BUSES DURING THE SECOND WORLD WAR. This picture shows the 'clippies' in front of the sea-front Bus Station.

THE REMAINS OF ORCHARD STREET after a night of bombardment, June 1942.

WAS THIS LITTLE BOY LOST OR DID HE JUST FIND IT ALL TOO TIRING? A 'Special' directs the traffic from the island at the junction of High Street, Regent Street and Meadow Street c. 1943.

Events

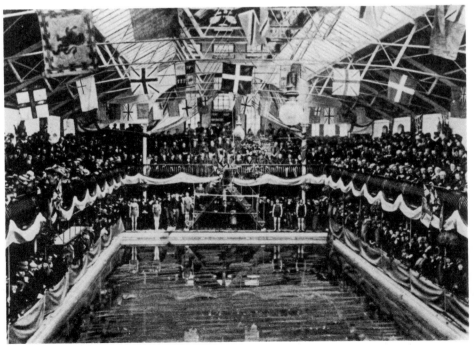

THE OPENING CEREMONY AT KNIGHTSTONE BATHS, 13 May 1902.

THE NORTHERN END OF THE HIGH STREET decorated for the Coronation of George V and Queen Mary in 1911.

MEADOW STREET, also decorated for the 1911 Coronation. On the left a man is selling fruit and vegetables from his barrow.

WILLIAM PARSONS with his donkey chair, decorated for the Coronation celebrations in 1911.

POST OFFICE STAFF line up for a special photograph to mark the Coronation of King George V and Queen Mary in 1911. The Head Postmaster, Tom Wills, is seated in the centre.

THE FIRST OF FOUR TRANS-ATLANTIC TELEGRAPH CABLES to be laid from Weston is brought ashore in this photograph of 1885. The cable ran from Weston to Waterville in Ireland and thence to St John, Newfoundland.

THE FIRST PILES are driven in for the new Grand Pier, November 1903.

GALES ON THE NIGHT OF 10 SEPTEMBER 1903 wreaked havoc in the town. Here the wooden bathing machines were wrecked beyond repair and were never replaced.

THIS PICTURE OF DAMAGE caused by the 1903 Great Gale shows the harbour wall at Knightstone, which collapsed.

For five years from 1919, Mr Frank Williams of Jubilee road would tour the town's streets at Christmas playing his 'fairy bells', to raise money for orphans of the First World War. George's Restaurant in the High Street, held the party in their hall and also collected toys from their customers so each child would receive a present. In this photograph the toys are being displayed before being distributed.

THE IRON SKELETON OF THE WINTER GARDENS PAVILION takes shape, 1926.

MESSRS ERNEST PALMER AND ERNEST MACFARLANE lead the procession of mayors at the opening of the Winter Gardens and Pavilion on 14 July 1927.

THE DUKE AND DUCHESS OF YORK (later King George VI and Queen Elizabeth) arrive at Weston-super-Mare Station on their way to open the new hospital on 6 July 1928. The Chairman of the UDC, Mr Ernest Macfarlane, is informing them that 2000 school children are about to sing the National Anthem.

THE SCENE IN THE BOULEVARD as the Duke and Duchess of York open the new hospital, 1928.

A SOUVENIR POSTCARD VIEW of the new Queen Alexandra Memorial Hospital, 1928.

DAVIES BROTHERS' SHOP in the High Street, decorated for the visit of the Duke and Duchess of York, 6 July 1928.

SECTION TWELVE

People

IVY JAMES (right) and her sister Maud, photographed by their father, William, on the steps of their home, Fortfield, 65 South Road in 1895.

STAFF AT WESTON-SUPER-MARE STATION, 1935. In the back row, left to right: —? —, —? — James Honeyset, Bernard Still, —? —? —? —, George Titt, Ralph Pike. In the middle row: —? —, Mr Hardcastle, —? —, Fred Howe, Mr Chalker, —? —, Fred Clarke, Mr More, —? —, James Palmer, Harry Mansbridge, Frank Coker, Jack Witheridge, Mr Holder, Charles Major, J. Burgoin (Station Master), —? —, —?, —, J.S. Cox, —? —, and in the front row: —? —, —? —, —? —, Miss Beaton, —? —, —? —, Edward Collins, —? —, and Fred Gundry.

F. POOLE. D. GILL. J. JAMES. E. E. BAKER H. F. DAVIES. J. SHORNEY. W. BOYDEN. H. PETHICK. W. DYER. S. HEAP. W. GALE. P. H. DEVERELL. T. PALMER.

C. MASTERS. W. H. BEEDLE. W. SMITH (Clerk). S. HARVEY (Chairman). S. C. SMITH (Deputy Clerk). J. PHILLIPS. S. TYLER.

WESTON-SUPER-MARE TOWN COMMISSIONERS AND LOCAL BOARD OF HEALTH in 1894. The photograph was taken by A. Legg outside Grove House in Grove Park.

'DAD' COMER was Weston's last Town Crier, working from 1915 until 1925, by which time he was aged 88. Still active, he went on to learn to drive a car. He died aged 91 from a fall from a ladder.

NURSE HAINES AND HER COLLECTORS, 1910. Seated is Daisy Riden and second from the right is Edie Major. Nurse Haines was a local midwife who set up a soup kitchen for the children of the poor.

CHILDREN QUEUING FOR SOUP TICKETS outside Nurse Haines' home in Alexandra Parade.

WESTON-SUPER-MARE LIFEBOAT CREW in the 1880s. In the back row, left to right are —?—,—?—,—?—, Alf Baker, —?—. In the middle row are John Hayden, —?—, Jack Glover, —?—, J. Tancock. In the front row is —?—, Jack Baker, Sam Doughty, —?—, and Alf Counsell.

THE BURNELL FAMILY AT WESTON STATION, 1896. From left to right is Olive (dressed in white), an aunt, Irene (the baby in the pram), Mrs Burnell, Rupert (who was to tragically die in the retreat from Mons in 1914) and a friend from London.

WESTON-SUPER-MARE VOLUNTEER FIRE BRIGADE, 1910. In the front row, left to right are Messrs Fry, T. Davey, —?—,Sims, —?—, Hillman, —?—. In the back row are Messrs Baker, —?—, W. Clarke, F. Allen, G. Bolton, Fred Day —?—, Pottenger and Hillman. Seated in the car is Dr Temple and Mr C. Croft.

THIS LITTLE GIRL JUST COULDN'T RESIST MAKING A SAND CASTLE (or is it a mud pie?) even though it is in the High Street. The hats are in Walker & Ling's window, 1909.

MR JACKSON BARSTOW AND FAMILY on their return from a motoring tour to the North of England. The car was one of two Daimler's owned by them. The chauffeur is Walter Burnell.

THREE LADIES REST FOR A WHILE in a seafront shelter on a winter's day in the 1890s.

ACKNOWLEDGEMENTS

My thanks must go firstly to Jane Evans, Curator of Woodspring Museum, for her help and for allowing me to draw extensively on the photographic collection at the Museum.

I would also like to thank Woodspring Central Library for permission to use several of their pictures and the archive department of Marks and Spencer PLC for searching out photographs of their Weston-super-Mare store.

The following individuals have generously lent photographs, and in many cases also supplied detailed information with them, therefore my thanks also go to Mr E. Amesbury, Brian Austin, Mrs Coles, Mrs M. Davies, Mrs Eler, Mrs Geeve, Lornie Leete-Hodge, Mr C. Lemon, Mr H. Major, Mr B. Middle, Mr J. Mullins, Mr D. Overy, Mrs Parsons, Mrs Phillips, Mrs Potter, Mr Prosser, Mrs Rendell and Mr Sinclair. I am also grateful to Mr M.J. Tozer for his assistance in dating some of the photographs of old transport.

The author: Sharon Poole has lived in Weston-super-Mare all her life and has worked at the Woodspring Museum for sixteen years. Sharon is especially responsible for the Social and Local History collections at the Museum and is herself a keen photographer, all of which makes her eminently suitable to compile this old photograph book.